WHY CHRISTIAN KIDS NEED A CHRISTIAN EDUCATION

Douglas Wilson

Why Christian Kids Need a Christian Education
Copyright © 2013 Athanasius Press
205 Roselawn
Monroe, Louisiana 71201
www.athanasiuspress.org

ISBN: 978-0-9842439-6-9 (softcover)

Quick Reference

Introduction

I am tempted to begin by arguing that Christian kids need Christian education because the point needs to be argued. They need a Christian education because *we* didn't get a Christian education, and look where we are. We didn't get a Christian education, and this is why it is necessary to explain to everybody why Christian kids need a Christian education.

But I resisted this temptation manfully. You don't persuade people who are on the fence by snarking at them. Isn't this true? You catch more flies with honey than with vinegar. But then, on the other hand, as a man once reasonably asked, who wants to catch flies?

There is actually another reason why I don't want to begin by arguing a point that is so obvious (but only to those for whom it is so obvious). Whenever sharp disagreements arise between Christians who are otherwise well-informed and well-intentioned, it is often wise to change the subject—or rather, to *appear* to change the subject. Earthquakes on the surface are caused by tectonic shifts well below the surface. Disagreements about things like the necessity of Christian education are actually disagreements about the nature of knowledge, the meaning of common grace, the authority of natural revelation, and the possibility of neutrality in education. These are the macro issues, and we will never get anywhere in our discussion of the details unless we address them first. These issues are the tectonic plates.

In order to discuss what a Christian school is supposed to do, we first have to settle what the Christian faith is supposed to do. In order to understand what Christian education is for, we have to determine what Christianity is for. We too often assume that we all agree on the role of Christianity, and then differences mysteriously arise when we get to the question of Christian education. However, the differences about education are usually differences that go all the way down. We argue about which map to use because of the differences we have over where we are supposed to go. The question of Christian education is therefore a litmus test—it reveals differences far greater than we initially thought were there.

If the Christian faith is all-encompassing, then of course Christian schools will fit naturally into that. But if the Christian faith is only supposed to apply to certain narrowly-defined aspects of life, then all-encompassing Christian schools will (naturally) be seen as examples of Christians over-reaching, meddling in things that are none of our business. The approach taken in this small book will therefore be to address some of these foundational theological issues first. Then, when those issues are laid out on the table in front of us, we may be able to make some progress in talking about the education of our children. If we can come to agree on the destination, we might have less trouble in our discussion of which map to use.

What is Education?

At the broadest level, education is the process of passing on to the next generation the parents' understanding of the nature of their world. When a Christian argues that it is not necessary to provide his children with an explicitly Christian education, he is *not* abandoning this definition of education. Rather, he is telling us something about *his* understanding of the nature of the world. He intends, just as much as anybody, to pass that understanding on to his children. The difference has to do with what that understanding actually is. He believes that a great deal of what we acquire in the process of education is "neutral," and he doesn't mind his children picking up a great deal of this neutral information—just as he did. He believes that *his* mind is filled with a great deal of that same kind of neutral information. He learns from non-believers, and why shouldn't his children do the same? Because he believes that the content of education contains a large amount of "neutral info," he also believes that it should be possible for Christian kids to get access that neutral info.

A Christian who thinks this way does not want his child to become a radical Muslim, a devout Buddhist, or an atheist. He wants his children to become *the same kind of Christian that he is*. He is carrying on a tradition that he has received, and is trying to do so faithfully. If that were not complicated enough, the other kind of Christian (the kind urging him to adopt a full-tilt Navy-Seals-for-Jesus approach) really is over-zealous sometimes. Such Christians often make true and biblical statements, but they sometimes don't know what spirit they are of (Luke 9:55). The claims of Christ—as I will be arguing—are in fact total. But these total claims don't just apply to Christians who have their kids in government schools. They also apply to the over-eager proselytizer, the one who turns people off unnecessarily. "Be not overly righteous, and do not make yourself too wise. Why should you destroy yourself?" (Ecc. 7:16). The total claims of Christ mean that sometimes those pressing those total claims need to lighten up.

This acknowledged, we may return to those Christian parents who believe there is such a thing as educational neutrality. This is not necessarily parental dereliction, but rather a particular doctrine of knowledge. That doctrine of knowledge is, I am convinced, harmful in the long run, but the Scriptures tell Christian teachers to refute false doctrine (Titus 1:9, 11), which is not the same thing as complaining about people who are following those unrefuted doctrines out.

10

The Bible tells us that we reap what we sow (Gal. 6:7), and if the church has not sown a thoroughly Christian view of epistemology, then how can we hope to reap a thoroughly Christian view of education? The field of epistemology asks how it is that we humans *know things*, and schools are places where young humans are coming to *know things*. The two issues are obviously related and intertwined. We cannot hope to come to an understanding of the second issue unless we resolve the first.

What Everybody Knows

In some respects, our present situation has come about because of the success of previous generations of Christian education. Because of the predominance of the gospel in the West for approximately a thousand years, there are a whole host of issues that we now just "take for granted." We think that these are things that "everybody just knows," when actually they are the fruit of a Christian worldview, extended over centuries. And when we say "everybody knows them," we *think* we mean Christian and non-Christian alike, but what we are actually referring to are Christians and non-Christians influenced by Christians. In other cases, we mean non-Christians who have been given a measure of common grace by God.

We naively believe that these common values are a shared inheritance among all humans, and whatever it was that Adam's fall into sin did, it did not erase these values. This means that it should be possible, or so the argument goes, to work together with non-believers in a task like education. Let's just seek out that common ground, and then work together. Why make this so complicated? Why make it so *sectarian*?

I said a moment ago that these common values are the fruit of a Christian worldview. "Nonsense!" someone might be tempted to reply. "*Everybody* knows that two plus two equals four, don't they?" Well, no, actually. The pantheists don't. How can two and two equal four when everything is actually *one*? There is no such thing as two—or four, for that matter. The postmodern relativists might stumble at a different spot. They don't have much of a problem with the twos and the fours, but they do have a problem asserting that such a proposition is *true*. How can something as simple as this be true when we don't have a basis for saying that *anything* is ultimately *true*? What is truth anyhow?

In short, it is easy to point to various worldviews that would answer the simplest questions differently. This would make it extraordinarily difficult to operate a school together with someone who did not share the same answers these questions. What we believe matters. Our religion affects the way we view the world, and the effect extends down to the fundamentals. It extends into the classroom, at every level.

One time I was part of a school board interviewing a young Christian graduate of a school of education at a nearby university. He wanted to teach at our school, and in order to test how effective his filters had been during the course of his studies, I asked him a question designed to reveal his understanding of the "look/say" method of teaching literacy. I asked him what he would do if he showed a student a paper that had the letters *h-o-r-s-e* on them, and the student read it aloud as *pony*. What would he do? Well, he said, without hesitation, he would praise the student. "Good job." Now this young man appeared to be a fine Christian in his dedication to Christ, but he did not know what it meant to *think* like a Christian in his chosen vocation. The premises from an alien religion were present here, skewing his answer.

Sometime after this, I was on a panel discussion at a conference on education, and I told this story. I also said, skylarking a bit with a *reductio ad absurdum*, that the time would come when math classes would be asking students what they wanted the sum of a particular math problem to equal. One of my fellow panelists was a math teacher from Canada, and he said that at his school this was no *reduction*, and no laughing matter. He said things were already at that crisis level at his school. You cannot deny the authority of truth and then evade the consequences of such a denial. You cannot chase truth away, and expect it to still be around.

The objection may be returned that this is simply playing "word games," and that the real issue is whether or not *any* nonbeliever can know these things, apart from faith in Jesus Christ. It is perhaps granted that *some* unbelievers don't know them, but what about the unbelievers who *do* know them? Doesn't that show that Christians and non-Christians *can* know something in common, without having to work through a statement of faith first? Someone doesn't have to affirm the Apostles' Creed to be able to affirm the truths of mathematics. This is quite true. There are men who cannot affirm the Creed together with me who nonetheless know a great deal more about the truths of God found in mathematics than I do. How is this possible? We have come to the point mentioned earlier—non-Christians influenced by Christians, or by the common grace of God Himself.

So what is this doctrine of common grace? This is the doctrine that allows us to recognize the insights, achievements, wisdom, and scholarship of unbelievers, and—this is the crucial point—to do so without granting the legitimacy of their idolatrous foundations. This is exactly the point at issue. When non-believers rebel against God, they do not lose everything all at once. They are not yet damned; they are not yet in the outer darkness.

Non-believers *do* know things, and they often know far more than believers do. How can this be harmonized with what we are saying here about the lordship of Jesus Christ over all knowledge? Think of it this way. In order to know what he does, the non-believer has to borrow premises from the Christian faith in order to get to the conclusions that he just somehow "knows." He may have received this common grace through his connection with a culture that was shaped by Christian doctrine, or he may have received it from God's natural revelation in the world at large. But either way, his correct conclusions do *not* follow from the premises dictated by *his* basic religious commitments.

For example, suppose that an atheist knows far more about microbiology than I do. He knows the ins and the outs on both sides of the cellular membrane, the names of all the mitochondrial parts, and which way the flagellum on the little bacterium rotates. I believe in Jesus, but I don't know any of that stuff. In short, he knows an enormous amount about how God's *design* at this level operates. But what he does not know is how to get all this micro-design from all his atheistic macro-chaos. He can't consistently get his knowledge from his premises about what the universe is like. He can't get that knowledge from his premises, but I can get *his* knowledge from *my* premises. This is why I can (and should) learn from unbelievers. I may glean knowledge from unbelievers, but what I must not take from them is their ignorance. I may plunder gold from the Egyptians, but this does not include the disconnect between their premises and their conclusion. That is not gold. They do *not* know that everything is time and chance acting on matter, and they cannot know that because it is not true. If they did know it, all the knowledge they have of microbiology would—*poof*—disappear.

Common grace is what happens when God allows non-believers to participate in and enjoy that which could not be true if their view of the universe were true. Common grace is the blessing that results when God allows non-believers to be inconsistent. If they were consistent, everything would come unstuck. It would all come apart in their hands. In order to know anything, they cannot be living in the universe they claim to be living in. So how is that they are frequently in line ahead of us? The answer is simple. They *cut*.

So with that stated, here is the difficulty. The government school system is not just one in which the true conclusions are taught, and where the false premises are ignored or given a miss. No, *the whole system is taught together*. The secular worldview is taught, top to bottom. This includes origins, the nature of knowledge, the progressive view of history, and so on. It is pretended that nothing is being said contrary to faith in Christ, or faith in Scripture. This is not quite true, but even if nothing whatever were ever explicitly said about Jesus or His Word, that silence would be thunderously loud. The child is learning that whatever you might believe about Jesus on your own time, His existence and attributes are irrelevant to the course of studies that the students are currently pursuing. How could this be possible? How could Jesus come back from the dead *in history*, and not alter the course and meaning of that history forever?

If a Christian kid is loyal enough to his parents to be motivated to do it, and bright enough to sort things out for himself, he may get through with his faith intact. He might *survive*. But your education is not something you are supposed to "survive." Your education is supposed to be your nourishment. You are not supposed to consider it a great victory if you "survive" breakfast.

"You shall not boil a young goat in its mother's milk" (Deut. 14:21b; Ex. 23:19; 34:26). The principle in this law is that we must not take that which was intended for the nourishment of life, and turn it into the instrument of death. A child's education ought to be like mother's milk to him. We must not take that which is intended for his nourishment and turn it into something that will be death to him.

Common grace comes in bits and pieces. Common grace does not provide a coherent system of belief, only with the Jesus part left out. Common grace is found in the midst of an idolatrous jumble. It is a good thing (comparatively) for unbelievers to receive because that jumble is to be preferred to the outer darkness. But the fact that God is being kind to unbelievers by holding them back from the full consequences of their rebellion does not mean that this jumbled and inconsistent curricular mishmash is suitable for the children of believers.

Humanity 2.0

John Dewey, the father of the modern American school system, objected to the essential divisiveness of orthodox Christianity. And, given his premises, he was quite right to object. A humanist is one who places ultimate value in the human race. Humanity, in essence, functions in the role of the divinity. But conservative Christians believe that the human race is actually divided into two groups—the saved and the lost. This division of the humanist deity was not to be tolerated. This is a theological difference that could not be papered over. The public schools were established in order to eradicate this difference, which actually amounts to the eradication of Christian education.

The final eschatology of the Christian faith (the issues of Heaven and Hell) dominates everything. If we believe that human history will culminate in a great judgment scene before the throne of God, where He will separate the sheep from the goats, then we believe something intolerable to the humanist. If we abandon this conviction, for the sake of peace with the humanists, we have not so much accomplished peace between Christians and humanists as we have left the Christian faith and gone over to the humanists.

There is no real way to "split the difference" between salvation and damnation. The gulf that separates the sheep and the goats is as great as the difference between Tolkien's orcs and elves. This means that believing Christians in the midst of the great humanist experiment (which is what their government school system *is*) will be Christians who are constantly getting under foot. They will constantly be getting in the way. They will ask questions which presuppose our final and respective destinations, and this will be intolerable. Or they will cease asking such questions, which means that the process of their corruption is well under way.

Heaven and Hell can be affirmed, ignored, or denied. Those who ignore this divide are simply in the early stages of denying it, but it is a relevant concern when it comes to many practical matters here and now. It is relevant to matters that come up in classrooms. When I was at the university (getting the kind of education I am arguing against here), we were once shown a film of a person who was diagnosed with a terminal and very painful disease. Rather than face the ravages of that disease, this person decided to commit suicide, and to make a film out of it. A party was thrown, at which all the farewells were said with the cameras running. The death was not shown on camera, but the film concluded after this poor individual had committed suicide. The entire rationale for this was the obvious need to avoid the excruciating pain of the disease in question. In our class discussion, I raised a question which was an alien concept for the others. I asked what basis we had for believing that the suicide in any way prevented pain. Hell is painful, far worse than whatever disease it was. But we were being asked to make an ethical calculation, and we were not allowed to bring in the possibility that the Christian faith might be true.

If the teaching of the Christian faith is true, God at the very beginning of our history established a foundational enmity between the seed of the woman and the seed of the serpent. "I will put enmity between you and the woman, and between your offspring and her off-spring; he shall bruise your head, and you shall bruise his heel" (Gen. 3:15).

This is the basis for the antithesis. If there is such an antithesis between faith and unbelief, an antithesis that cuts across the board, then how could there *not* be such an antithesis between faithful education and unbelieving education? If there is such a dividing line throughout all of life, then how could there not be such a dividing line throughout preparation for that life? If God's purpose is to grow us up into a perfect man (Eph. 4:13), then should we not be bending everything we do toward that final end or purpose? And should this not include the education of our children?

When the Bible teaches that Jesus Christ is the last Adam (Rom. 5:14; 1 Cor. 15:45), we have to realize what this means. Adam means *mankind*, which means that Jesus Christ is the new humanity. He is the last mankind. We have the privilege of growing up into Him, but this is not going to be accomplished by fits and starts. We are not going to grow up into the perfect man in fits of absentmindedness. This is the end goal for all our discipleship—a discipleship that should include schools for our children.

What a Worldview Actually Is

Over the last thirty years, many Christians have thankfully been encouraged to "think Christianly." There has been quite an explosion of various publications and worldview seminars, all designed to help Christians push the ramifications of their faith into the corners. This is all to the good. But a Christian worldview—while it must include how we think—is not *limited* to how we think.

Worldviews are inescapable, and every tribe, nation, and people in the history of the world have always had them, though we only started talking about it in the late eighteenth century. The first person to use the word (*weltanschauung*) was the philosopher Immanuel Kant. By this, he simply meant "sense perception of the world." But the word caught on for some reason (don't you find yourself just *wanting* to say *weltanschauung* yourself from time to time?), and almost immediately after this, other philosophers picked it up and began using it in a sense more familiar to us—meaning "framework of assumptions about the world." Throughout the course of the nineteenth century, the idea was important to philosophers like Hegel, Kierkegaard, and Nietzsche. Conservative Christians soon picked up the idea to advance the idea of a fully-orbed Christian take on the world. This was done by James Orr and Abraham Kuyper, carrying us over into the early twentieth century. The most recent round of play was initiated in the 1970s by Francis Schaeffer, who was largely responsible for making the word and concept a commonplace in evangelical circles

It is commonly assumed that a worldview simply consists of "what and how you think." Thus it is assumed that you can therefore get a Christian worldview out of a book, or send your kids to two weeks of intensive worldview training in the summer. Some Christian parents think that this is the task of Christian schools. Such things are not necessarily bad, of course, at least as far as they go, but what *is* bad is the idea that a worldview consists of nothing more than propositional answers to questions.

Think of a full Christian worldview as a wheel, with our propositional answers to the basic questions as just one of the four spokes. This is the element most people think of when they think worldview. How do you answer the ultimate questions? What do you think is true about the world? Example: "Christian, what do you believe?" "I believe in God the Father Almighty." Competing example: "All that appears to be reality is actually *maya*, illusion, and all things are ultimately one." In a solid Christian school, this doctrinal element is taught and instilled. Let us call this spoke *catechesis*. It is what the kids would get from the Bible class, or the chapels and assemblies.

Then there is *lifestyle*. How do we actually live? This is the second spoke. How do you conduct business? Do you work hard? Do you live in kindness? What kind of clothes do you wear? What kind of music do you sing and listen to? Example: "We would really love to get a modest but lovely dress for the protocol dinner." Competing example: "Do you have any of those mud-flaps with the silhouette girls on them?" In a good Christian school, the lifestyle issue is embedded in the culture of the school. In a poor Christian school, the lifestyle element of a Christian worldview is buried under legalistic rules, or any attempt to live out a distinctively Christian lifestyle is just abandoned. With the former error, the school is likely to be a small, fundamentalist school. With the latter error, it is likely to be a prep school with high academics and high levels of worldliness. In a good school, there will be a shared set of behavioral expectations—from entertainment standards to dating partners, and from dating partners to academic honesty.

The third spoke would be something called *narrative*. What kind of story do you tell yourself? Where do you and your family fit into the story? Who are your people? What relationship do they have to all of God's people? Example: "The Puritans came to New England because they wanted freedom to worship." Competing example: "Many millions of years ago, the primordial ooze was poised for a major breakthrough." A Christian school provides an outstanding opportunity for a student to learn how to identify with his people, including "his people" who may belong to a different denomination. They are still your people.

The fourth spoke is symbol, or liturgy. How do you summarize and ritually enact your basic commitments? Example: canceling school because of Good Friday. Competing example: saying the Pledge of Allegiance at every basketball game. It's a Christian league. Why not say the Apostles' Creed first? It can't be because reciting something over and over like that makes it meaningless—that would mean the Pledge is meaningless. But if you seriously propose that it be dropped, you will find out how "meaningless" it is. Ritual really is powerful, and a good Christian school has many solid opportunities to reinforce this spoke as well.

Two of these spokes—catechesis and narrative—depend upon the use of language. For the sake of brevity, and because the elements of lifestyle and ritual grow up out of these two, we will focus on them.

The fact that we confess something with our mouth (and that doing so is essential to salvation) means that we do presuppose certain things about language. Language is a trustworthy gift from a trustworthy God; it is not an evolutionary by-product. Adam was created speaking. Our toddlers are born as naming creatures, and they grow up into it. This is also the grace of God.

Now what should we do with grace? What are we to do with a gift? We are simply to receive it, with gratitude. We are not to over-analyze it. We are not to over-engineer it. We must not become victims of a false analogy. It is wrong-headed to say that "we build telescopes, but cannot see God. We build listening devices, but cannot hear God. We invent languages, but cannot talk with or about God." It is false to say that we invented the idea of propositions; they are the sheer grace of God—whether we want to say *the magazine is on the end table* or *Jesus is Lord of heaven and earth*.

The same thing is true of narrative, or story-telling. In His parables, Jesus is frequently retelling the story of the history of Israel. He does so in a way that challenges the current corruptions of that generation, but also does so in a way that reveals He is dealing with the entire history of Israel. He does it in a way that subverts the common assumptions. We frequently miss this because we are not steeped in the imagery of the Old Testament. We don't know what images, motifs, and symbols are being drawn on. Imagine someone today telling a story in which we were to find alabaster cities, fruited plains, and bald eagles. *Those* allusions would not be lost on us. The vineyard, according to the Jews' understanding of themselves, was Israel (Is. 5:1; Ps. 80:15).

The point in this is not that story-telling is a sign of mental health (although it is), or that well-adjusted people love stories (although they do). The point is that narrative is an inescapable element in all worldviews. It is not something you ought to have; it is something you will have, regardless. What you ought to have is the *right* story, not just *a* story. You can no more be without a narrative of "where you are" than you can be without a beating heart. So the issue is not storytelling or not, but rather faithful storytelling versus unfaithful storytelling.

At the macro level, there are two great errors with regard to this. The first is the error of modernity, which likes to pretend that Science is all we need, and that storytelling is for the simpler ones among us, who need to be periodically amused. But despite their pretensions, they still tell us *their* story of how science delivered us from medieval superstitions, they tell us how we evolved from the primordial goo, they tell us how the evolution of the secular state delivered us from religious fundamentalism and its ugly twin, fanaticism.

The second great problem is the idea that storytelling is the individual's prerogative, in order to express his inner, creative artesian well. This radical privatizing of storytelling is a great tragedy. This really does reduce storytelling to the level of private amusement. Great stories belong to a people, just as great creative geniuses do. Stories are a corporate affair, which means that schools are a natural place for them. If there were more wholesome stories in our Christian schools, there would be more students who wanted to be there.

God has given us *the* story. God has given us a Book that reveals His mind to us. Most of this book consists of stories, not didactic outlines. A significant portion of the remainder of the Bible is poetry. The same fundamental story is told over and over again, in astonishingly different ways, and yet in a way that leaves us with the unmistakable sense that we are being taught how we are to live. We do this by hearing the story, internalizing it. We are to be Bible readers, Bible listeners, Bible tellers. When we walk along the road, when we rise up, when we lie down. We point to the moon and we tell our kindergartener the story of how it got there.

We do this, in the second place, by seeing ourselves in the story. We do this by seeing ourselves (our people) in the early chapters, those already written. We also do this by seeing Scripture as the first four chapters, and the history of the Church is the fifth chapter—the story is still being written. We refuse to separate history from story, an evil suggestion from the dragon, and if we told more of the right kind of story, we would know what to do with dragons.

Third, we are then to tell our own stories, drawing on the stock of images, phrases, motifs, themes, and structures that we find in the Bible. The Christian imagination cannot be free until it is captured by the Scriptures and by the Spirit of God. When it is, the world will stand back in amazement. This is because, at bottom, Christians are the only people with a genuine story. *Christian students in Christian schools have to be taught how to tell it.*

The story line is this: grace, envy, sin, promise, sacrifice, resurrection, and fulfillment. We have Eden, the Fall, Cain, the coming Messiah, the Cross, the Resurrection, and Glory. We have Faithful dying in Vanity Fair. We have the Stone Table and the shorn mane. We have the battle of Helm's Deep. We have Ransom calling down the powers of deep heaven. We have Roland and St. George, Beowulf and Dante. We have Br'er Rabbit, and we have the man who was Thursday. Beyond them all, we have the parables of Jesus, stories that would reward much more careful attention.

Everything in the "biblical worldview" can be "just right," right on paper, that is, and yet everything can still be wrong. Your doctrine can be right, your ethical standards can be right, your liturgy can be right, and your narrative can be right. But if love, joy, peace, patience, and so on, do not suffuse the whole of it, then it is a caricature of the biblical worldview, and not the authentic thing. The grace of God invades the world, *and it changes things*. If we cannot get away from the grace of God in "the spokes," then the sinful heart tries to keep the axle from turning in such a way that requires the spokes to move. Christ Himself is the axle and all four spokes have to be embedded in Him.

Without grace, propositional affirmation is the devil's religion (Jas. 2:19). Without grace, lifestyle standards are just suffocating moralism (Matt. 23:4). Without grace, liturgy is mumbo-jumbo and parading about (Amos 5:21–24). Without grace, storytelling confounds the protagonist and antagonist (John 8:39). And with all these things, apart from grace, the "better" it is, the worse it is. Appealing to the argument, or the rules, or the tradition, or history is all worthless apart from the experienced and tasted goodness of God. This means joy—joy in the doctrine, joy in the living, joy in the worship and symbols, and joy in the story. The joy of the Lord is our strength.

Two of these spokes involve actions, not words. The two others involve words, not actions. Lifestyle and liturgy are enacted. Stories and doctrines are spoken or written. All four enter their glory when they are done, or told, *from the heart*. Stories are no more protected from becoming a series of abstractions than catechism answers are. Both are propositional. Lifestyle is no more protected from becoming an empty drill than liturgy is. The issue is therefore not what spoke we prefer, or what emphasis we think needs to be restored, but whether God is pouring out His grace or not. Reformation is entirely and completely dependent upon the grace of God, and whether or not He bestows it is entirely up to Him.

We cannot create this axle, and we cannot (by arranging or juggling the spokes) connect them to the axle. Reformation is the work of God. But *when* He works, this is what it looks like. When He works, that work will include a proliferation of Christian schools that help parents grow the next generation up into a full-orbed Christian worldview, a worldview that encompasses all of life.

Every Thought Captive

We cannot accept a view of the world in which certain things are considered under the lordship of Christ, while other things are allowed to drift off by themselves, untethered. There must be an integration point. Now we have already noted that Christ is "the axle," and while it sounds very pious, what does it mean?

> For though we walk in the flesh, we are not waging war according to the flesh. For the weapons of our warfare are not of the flesh but have divine power to destroy strongholds. We destroy arguments and every lofty opinion raised against the knowledge of God, and take every thought captive to obey Christ. (2 Cor. 10:3–5)

The knowledge of God is declared in all things. Every blade of grass, every mountain range, every galaxy, pours forth speech. This means that botany, geology, and astronomy are all, when rightly understood, disciplines that must bend the knee to Christ. If they do not, then they are what Paul calls "lofty opinions," and it is our task to take them captive to Christ. "Great are the works of the LORD, *studied* by all who delight in them" (Ps. 111:2). This is a conclusion that can only be escaped by someone who has decided (somewhat arbitrarily) that epistemological dualism is an option. Epistemological schizophrenia would be more like it.

> And he is before all things, and in him all things hold together. And he is the head of the body, the church. He is the beginning, the firstborn from the dead, that in everything he might be preeminent. (Col. 1:17–18)

For the Christian, Christ is to have preeminence in all things. Note that He is not to have the preeminence in all *spiritual* things, or in all *theological* things. Christ is not quarantined anywhere. He is the Lord, and this means He is the Lord of all. This is the fundamental Christian confession (Rom. 10:9). When we confess Him as Lord of theology, but not of history, or Lord of my heart, and not of my head, then this is simply a clever way of denying Him. This is just as bad a confessing Him to be the Lord of the mountains, but not of the plains (1 Kings 20:23). That is the kind of mistake that pagans make. If Jesus is only Lord here, then He is not Lord at all. If Jesus is not the Lord *of* all, then He is not the Lord *at* all.

When Paul says here that Christ is to have preeminence in all things, he says this for a particular reason. Jesus is before all history, and is therefore Lord of all history. He is before all things—and this means all things are shaped and created by Him, *and not the other way around.*

In Him all things hold together. What does this mean? Jesus did not just create the cosmos (John 1:3), but He also sustains it. It came into being as a result of His powerful word, and it continues to sustain its existence solely because He continues to speak.

> Long ago, at many times and in many ways, God spoke to our fathers by the prophets, but in these last days he has spoken to us by his Son, whom he appointed the heir of all things, *through whom also he created the world.* He is the radiance of the glory of God and the exact imprint of his nature, *and he upholds the universe by the word of his power.* (Heb. 1:1–3a)

He created the world (Heb. 1:2), and He keeps the world created by His speaking (Heb. 1:3). If Jesus ceased to speak the world, the entire cosmos would go *ffwwiiip,* and be done. That's exactly the sound it would make too, only really fast.

So when Paul in Colossians says that all things are "held together" by Christ, he means much more than that all things "make sense" because of Jesus. Yes, all things do make sense because of Him, but this is not "a sense" that is superimposed on reality after the fact. Christ makes sense of the world precisely because He *is* the sense of the world.

This is why studying the world "objectively," without reference to Christ, is like trying to put the sun out so you can study the world more objectively. Studying in the dark is not objective; it is stupid.

Paul also tells us in the Colossians passage that Christ is the head of His body, which is the Church. He goes further and says that Christ is the *arche* (translated here as *beginning*). But the word *arche* refers to more than just the chronological starting point. Christ is the integration point for all things. We know these things concerning Him because He came back from the dead, as the firstborn from among the dead. Now if a man comes back from the dead, after three days in the tomb, how would it be possible for Him *not* to be the Lord of all education?

Further, how is it possible for men to claim that they believe that He did in fact come back from the tomb, and yet subsequently argue that this does not change absolutely everything? The writers of the New Testament knew what the resurrection meant. It meant, fundamentally, that Jesus Christ had to be granted the preeminence in everything. When I say *everything*, I mean every blessed thing. This includes, necessarily, the process of education. The risen Christ of the New Testament *defines everything*.

Now it is quite possible for a man to conclude that he does not believe all these things about Jesus. It is possible for a man to want his Jesus to be a delimited Jesus, suitable for mounting on the dashboard of his car. He might want a Jesus who is a *subset* of everything that is, instead of the Lord and sustainer of everything that is. He may choose that Jesus if he wishes, but he should know that it is not the Jesus described in the New Testament. It would also probably be for the best if such a man stopped calling himself a Christian.

God's Two Books

What about natural revelation? Some Christians are troubled by the fact that "natural revelation" sometimes appears to contradict "special revelation." When this happens, does not intellectual honesty require us to accept the findings of science? And if doing this conflicts with certain traditional readings of Scripture, should not those traditional readings give way? If we build schools that are "biblically absolutist" in the way I appear to be describing here, would this not result in us bringing our children up to be intellectually lazy and dishonest? Why would Jesus want us to do something like that?

A common contemporary example of this is Darwinism, and a salutary warning from the past to all fundamentalists everywhere is the disastrous treatment that Galileo got from the hidebound conservatives of his day, who refused to read Scripture in the new light that science was providing. They stuck to their geocentric guns, and tried to make the faith a laughingstock. We are still having to deal with the consequences of their obscurantism, and it has been centuries now.

The incident with Galileo is indeed salutary, and provides an outstanding example for us today when considering the claims of things like Darwinism. But in order for us to take that lesson, it is necessary for us to know something about history, and not just theology and science. The Church of that day was geocentric, not because a close study of Scripture demanded it, but rather because the best *science* of the day demanded it. The Church was not caught in a bind between Bible and Science, but was rather caught in a bind between the Old Science and the New Science. As someone has wisely said, one who marries the science of the day today should be prepared to be a widow tomorrow. More than one reader of this small book has been called an idiot for not accepting something taught in the current textbooks, and now, twenty years later, those textbooks have all been discarded and replaced—but somehow we who remain dubious remain idiots. The textbooks may come and go, but while they are here we must apparently believe in them with all our hearts.

Aristotle taught a geocentric view of things, and Aristotle was accepted as the authority. His was a secular authority; he was a *pagan*. The Church accepted the science of the day, and everybody who was anybody would have laughed them to scorn had they not done this. Now, once this cosmology was accepted on Aristotle's say-so, because they were professing Christians who had done this, some ingenuity was expended to find verses that would back all this up. Aristotle said that the earth was at the center, and so here we find (surprise!) a verse that says the same thing: "From the rising of the sun to its setting, the name of the LORD is to be praised!" (Ps 113:3). How do you like *them* apples?

The situation is exactly analogous to those day-agers who have studied the first two chapters of Genesis in the hopes of finding some room for geology in there. If the first two chapters of Genesis were a wet washcloth, certain exegetes have managed to wring millions of years out of them so far. This is not a collision between science and the Scriptures. Rather, this is the technique of those in the grip of the latest ephemeral vapor trying to hold onto a vague inspirational meaning for the Bible at the same time.

God has indeed written two books—General Revelation and Special Revelation. General revelation is in fact *revelation* (Ps. 19:2–3; Rom. 1:19–20), and Scripture is special revelation, more precise revelation, revelation given to us in the form of language. We should read both of these books as coming from the same Author, but we should do so remembering one of the fundamental laws of hermeneutics. The unclear passage must be interpreted in the light of the clear one, and not the other way around. Before we can read both of these books, we have to learn *how* to read them. And teaching people to read is one of the things that Christian schools do very well.

A Theology of Children

Having considered the nature of the world, we must also consider the nature of our children. Education, like everything else we undertake, has countless methods we can get tangled up in. Whatever methods we choose, we must pursue them in faith. But in order for our faith to be well grounded, we have to build on what God has actually said.

Covenant keeping cannot be done by our works, or any autonomous effort that we might supply. Covenant keeping is promise believing—nothing more, and nothing less. But many of the promises given to us by God are promises that concern our children. This means that numerous covenant promises are promises concerning the process of education. At the center of these promises, God offers us the salvation of our children. Now the only way to apprehend this kind of promise is by faith.

The faith that apprehends such promises is a gift from God, and the only kind of faith that God gives is a living faith. God only gives the kind of faith that is capable of receiving His remaining gifts. God gives us hands so that He may then give us all the remaining presents.

Now rigorous Christian education (with regard to the curriculum on paper) can be established, maintained and encouraged in a spirit of unbelief. In short, it is possible to have our lips approach God and yet have our hearts remain far from Him. This approach was discovered by Cain, the third human being ever. Adam and Eve discovered disobedience, but they also discovered repentance. Cain discovered false repentance and false worship, and people have been offering strange fire ever since.

Even though the outside of the cup can be washed without affecting the inside, the reverse is not true. Whenever the inside of the cup is washed, the outside will also be clean, as Jesus taught (Matt. 23:26). And so if we believe God concerning our children, this will necessarily result in rigorous Christian education.

Use the illustration of farming. If God promised a farmer a glorious harvest, and he really believed the promise, this would not induce him to stay home instead of plowing and planting. And it would be wrongheaded to accuse him of unbelief because he was out there plowing and planting—even though his neighbors are also plowing and planting precisely because they are trusting in themselves, and not in God.

Those unhappy Christian parents who believe that the beneficial results of education are somehow "up to them" will often be frantic in their pursuit of educational resources, ideas, and schools. The parents who believe

God will not answer this problem by lounging about, eating grapes. They will work also, just as hard. But a vast chasm separates faith working its way out in love and unbelief trying to fill up their covenantal black hole with autonomous human striving.

All this is to say that godly Christian education is impossible apart from a right mind about the covenant and a sane heart with regard to faith and works. In order to do this rightly we should have a robust theology of children.

If we are convinced that the world must be understood in a distinctively Christian way, then it makes sense that we believe young saints are to be trained up into that way of thinking about it. They are in the world God made, and we believe that they should be taught to line up with it. The reason the world must be understood in a Christian way is because the world was created by the Christian God. Apart from Him, it cannot be understood properly.

Because of the presence of sin in the world, there are a great many obstacles to this proper understanding. Children in Christian schools are not just Christians. They are also fallen; they are also sinners. Understanding does not come easily. Education is all about learning how to take your rightful place in the world, and this is something too important to leave to our young people to figure out for themselves, especially when there are obstacles everywhere—obstacles set by the world, the flesh, and the devil. Discipleship does not begin when a child reaches the age of eighteen. The Christian faith is not like one of those rides at Disneyland, where you have to be a certain height to participate. The enemy of their souls doesn't wait until they are eighteen. Why should we?

45

This should be thought of as more of a cultural expectation, and not as a "legalistic requirement." We know that there difficult circumstances where Christian education is impossible (*e.g.*, where children are assigned to a government school as a result of a court order in a divorce case). Nevertheless, Christian education is something we are striving to provide for all our covenant children and if, for example, someone's financial circumstances make private education unattainable, we want to have financial assistance available through the church and its deacon fund.

We should consider this to be part of our life together. When a child is baptized, it is common for the congregation to be presented with a question that has the force of an oath. "Do you as a congregation undertake the responsibility of assisting these parents in the Christian nurture of this child? If so, then signify by saying *amen*." Before saying *amen* to such a question, it is important to have a theology of children that allows for and requires it. To the basis of such a theology, we may now turn.

Nurture and Admonition

Now we are able to come to the point where we can cite scriptural passages on the subject of education proper, and have them seem pertinent. Let's say there was a passage that said outright that Christian kids should receive a Christian education. If we had begun our discussion by quoting that passage to someone who differed, we would have moved straight to the disagreement. But *why* was there disagreement? We had to deal with the paradigms that were operating below the surface first. If we do not do that, then when one person quotes the verse, the other person says that this is not the way he interprets it. He doesn't "see it that way." Right, but why?

Having addressed those paradigmatic questions first, we are now in a position to show how Scripture *does* require covenant education for covenant children.

> "Now this is the commandment, the statutes and the rules that the LORD your God commanded me to teach you, that you may do them in the land to which you are going over, to possess it, that you may fear the LORD your God, you and your son and your son's son, by keeping all his statutes and his commandments, which I command you, all the days of your life, and that your days may be long. Hear therefore, O Israel, and be careful to do them, that it may go well with you, and that you may multiply greatly, as the LORD, the God of your fathers, has promised you, in a land flowing with milk and honey. "Hear, O Israel: The LORD our God, the LORD is one. You shall love the LORD your God with all your heart and with all your soul and with all your might. And these words that I command you today shall be on your heart. You shall teach them diligently to your children, and shall talk of them when you sit in your house, and when you walk by the way, and when you lie down, and when you rise." (Deut. 6:1–7)

Jesus tells us that this passage contains the greatest commandment to be found in the entire Old Testament (Matt. 22:36-37). It is worth noting that the context of this commandment is a passage that is insisting on the necessity of covenant education. The law of God—His commandments, statutes, and rules—are to be lived out in the land the Israelites were entering (v. 1). The law that was to be taught was not a narrow doctrinal catechism. It was not a just Sunday School curriculum. It was an education for *life*. The intention was for them to teach these requirements to their sons and their grandsons (v. 2). A blessing was promised to them if they do so (v. 3). Then the great *Shema* was given to them—the Lord our God, the Lord is one (v. 4). The great commandment was then delivered to them. Love the Lord your God with all your heart, all your soul, and with all your might (v. 5). This does not just simply mean they were to love God "a lot." Jesus interprets in a more all-encompassing way—He adds the element of *mind*. You shall love the Lord your God with all your *brains* (Matt. 22:37). In short, the people of God are to love God (and are to teach their children and grandchildren to love God) *with everything they have and are.* Where in this is room for us to discover a neutral zone of activity in which love for God is unnecessary? No . . . if men can do it, then they need to learn how to do it in the love of God. Since we must love God in all things, this means we must learn how to love God in all things. And this means a believing education.

This includes (obviously) history, grammar, mathematics, science, geography, literature, and so on, through the rest of the entire curriculum.

> Give ear, O my people, to my teaching; incline your ears to the words of my mouth! I will open my mouth in a parable; I will utter dark sayings from of old, things that we have heard and known, that our fathers have told us. We will not hide them from their children, but tell to the coming generation the glorious deeds of the LORD, and his might, and the wonders that he has done. He established a testimony in Jacob and appointed a law in Israel, which he com-

manded our fathers to teach to their children, that the
next generation might know them, the children yet
unborn, and arise and tell them to their children, so
that they should set their hope in God and not forget
the works of God, but keep his commandments; and
that they should not be like their fathers, a stubborn
and rebellious generation, a generation whose heart
was not steadfast, whose spirit was not faithful to
God. (Ps. 78:1–8)

The remainder of this psalm addresses the problems
that were caused when the people of Israel *did not remember* what God had done for them. They did not remember over the course of generations, which means
that they had a failure in their system of education. God
has every expectation that when He does something for
a people that they in turn will teach their children about
it. There is a relationship between God's deliverances in
history, and a people's willingness to obey His commandments. It is no coincidence that we in this nation
have wandered from God's law—as a nation we wandered first from a recollection of what He did for us.

Let us suppose for just a moment that the triune God
acted in marvelous ways two and half centuries ago, and
that He established our nation with the strength of His
right arm. Suppose He did that, and that our fathers at
the time recognized it. Should the memory of these great
acts of His be perpetuated and kept alive and entrusted
to a school system that defiantly refuses, as a matter of
principle, to believe in Him? It makes a difference
whether Moses or Jeroboam writes the history curriculum (Lev. 11:45; 1 Kings 12:28). Which gods brought Israel out of the land of Egypt? Should that question be

answered by disinterested historians, pretending to be objective? Apart from the problem of there being no such thing, would such men provide God-honoring answers for us even if they did exist?

The thought experiment is more than just an interesting supposal. Horace Walpole said that cousin America had run off with a Presbyterian parson, referring to Witherspoon. One of the names for the War for Independence in England was The Presbyterian Revolt. At Yorktown, when Cornwallis surrendered to Washington, all of the colonels in Washington's army (with one exception) were elders in Presbyterian churches. Over fifty percent of the Continental Army were Presbyterians. The rest were Congregationalists and Baptists, and everybody was a Calvinist. Presbyterian ministers were known as the Black Regiment because of their black Genevan gowns that they wore when preaching. From this we may conclude—as Jeroboam so aptly summarized it—that all the Founding Fathers were Deists. *It makes a difference who writes the history curriculum.*

"The fear of the LORD is the beginning of knowledge; fools despise wisdom and instruction" (Prov. 1:7). We have already seen how "knowledge" should not be bifurcated into two sections—"spiritual knowledge" over here, and the rest of regular old knowledge over there. Knowledge is knowledge, and the fear of the Lord is the beginning of it. We should immediately see how this is important for the process of education. The very next verse addresses the recipient of the book of Proverbs—"*Hear, my son*, your father's instruction, and forsake not your mother's teaching, for they are a graceful garland for your head and pendants for your neck" (Prov. 1:8–9).

The book of Proverbs is a book of instruction in wisdom for a believer's son. While the book does contain what we would consider devotional material, in a biblical framework this kind of thing is not isolated from earthy, practical knowledge. If they had had cars back then, we wouldn't be surprised to find Proverbs advising us to rotate our tires, and change our oil every 3,000 miles. Part of this young man's curriculum includes learning to not cosign notes (Prov. 6:1–5), principles of political science (Prov. 28:16), economics (Prov. 10:22; 14:23; 20:10), conflict management (Prov. 15:1), business management (Prov. 22:29), and countless other topics. According to one understanding of spirituality, Proverbs is not a very spiritual book. But according to another more accurate understanding, we come to know that *true spirituality encompasses everything*. That being the case, a Christian education in all things becomes necessary.

In his letter to the Ephesians, the apostle Paul says this. "Fathers, do not provoke your children to anger, but bring them up in the discipline and instruction of the Lord" (Eph. 6:4).

There are two important words here, and each of them refers to the process of what we would call *education*. The first is discipline, translating the Greek word *paideia*. The second word, translated instruction, is *nouthesia*. The apostle is telling the fathers of Ephesus to teach their children in accordance with the precepts of the Lord. This phrase *of the Lord* is not a limiting phrase, as though there were some aspects of life that had nothing to do with Him, but then, when we get to the Sunday School lessons, we have to make sure that instruction is "of the Lord." No, the Greek word *paideia* is a much broader word than that.

Every language has what might be called common nouns—boots and chairs, and things like that. But every culture also has what we might call laden nouns, nouns which point to something of great importance in that society. In our culture, a word like *democracy* would fit that description, while *slippers* would not. In the Greco-Roman culture, the word *paideia* was like the word *democracy* in range and importance. It referred to the entire process of enculturation, as a child was rooted in the way of life established by his fathers. *Paideia* was enculturation, and a *paideia* "of the Lord" is therefore a *Christian* enculturation. It is nothing less than a Christian education, one that presupposes a Christian culture for the young child to be grown up into. If we do not have such a Christian culture, then the obvious thing to do is . . . build one. So, if anything, our word *education* is too small for it—referring, as it sometimes does, to what happens at the school building between 8 and 3. But if you take it in its broadest meaning—education for life, in all of life, we are getting close.

Christendom Lite

The government schools today are bastions of unbelief. The fact that many Christians do not see the problem with having their children there represents an intellectual and spiritual disconnect, but it is not a disconnect that happened all at once. The thing has developed gradually.

Seventy-five years ago, the public schools in the Bible belt were recognizably part of what could be described as Christendom Lite. The schools were dominated by a generally Christian ethos, and, at the same time, those schools were integrated fully into the broader society—the schools were part of the same society that contained the feed store, the churches, the theater, and so on. The defenders of the schools as they now exist are making a mistake, but they rightly see the attack on the schools as an attack on the way of life that encompasses all of society.

Their mistake is in failing to recognize that the Christian element, long weak but still there, has been almost completely diluted by the secularists.

In response to this, many clear-thinking Christians want to pull out and establish rigorously Christian schools. They are to be praised for this, but unfortunately a number of them have a sectarian vision for it. In other words, they want isolated (and pure) Christian schools. The defenders of the public schools in the Bible belt want schools that are integrated with all of society. In this, they have the more biblical position. The former are more biblical in their insistence that education be *explicitly* Christian. The latter are more biblical in their insistence that education be integrated with society at large. What we need to recover is a vision that combines *both* these perspectives.

So then, our children need to be educated in a robust, Trinitarian way. This is not an option or an add-on. At the same time, our vision should be for the schools that we establish to be the schools that serve at the center of our (evangelized) communities. Christian education is too important to be exiled to the edge of town. We do not want Christendom Stout sold only in hard-to-find micro-breweries. Neither do we want Christendom Lite in aisle 7 of every supermarket. We want Christendom, and we know that Christendom needs many really fine Christian schools.

Sin and the Christian School

One common objection to Christian schools is that it results in "hothouse" Christians. Do the kids ever learn to really stand up to sin? Are they growing to maturity in an artificial environment of godliness? And doesn't this mean they are not growing up to maturity at all? It is true that one trap that Christian school parents fall into is the trap of not wanting any sin at all around their kids. But I suppose this requires some explanation.

The mistake arises because there are a bunch of sinners that parents *should* keep away from their kids—kidnappers, for starters, and cocaine dealers, and pornographers, and seducers, and Cartesian dualists. One of the accusations leveled against private Christian education is that conservative parents are sheltering their kids. What next?! Parents sheltering children! We feed them too.

But here is where the mistake comes in. There is a question of degree here. We are *not* supposed to keep our children away from the presence of all sin whatever. And that's a good thing, too, because it is impossible. There is a type of sin, common to the human condition, that your children will encounter (on a daily basis) on the playground of the finest Christian school imaginable. If you refuse to send your kids to that school (because of all the sin there), then they will encounter even more of it at church, in their relationships with their siblings, in their bedroom all alone, and in the midst of all the dirty little thoughts between their ears. The task of Christian parents here is not to avoid this kind of sin, but rather to teach their children how to battle it. You cannot learn to battle something if you are constantly endeavoring to stay away from it. Running away is not the best strategy here.

In short, with this kind of sin, there are two errors—equally bad. One is to accommodate yourself to the presence of this kind of room temperature sin, in such a way as to assume room temperature yourself. That is the way of spiritual death. The other is to pretend to yourself that the choices you have made have somehow successfully distanced you from all that icky stuff. But it is as close to you now as it ever was, but is now invisible because you have daubed your eyes with a special Pharisee salve. This is another way of spiritual death.

The mere *presence* of sin discredits nothing and no one. A school is not a poor school because junior high girls are catty at lunch, because one of the boys in the fourth grade makes earthy observations about certain bodily functions, or because some cute blonde named Kimberly gets great grades and the word among the kids in the back row who don't like to study is that she might be the teacher's pet. Welcome to earth, everybody. This is not the kind of sin parents are required to keep their kids away from. They are in fact required *not* to try. This is the kind of sin that parents need to teach their kids to handle, and *avoidance is not a biblical strategy*. Because it will be necessarily unsuccessful, avoidance is simply a pretense of avoidance, with the down side— because you are too busy kidding yourself—of having children who are not learning how to respond and resist.

Suppose your child is in the classroom of a fine Christian school, one with a great reputation. You know the teachers and administrators, and they really love the Lord. But you know for a *fact* that two/thirds of the kids in your son's class are all hot about the latest skanky movie. Just last night, after the youth group get-together, they all went to see *Skanky Movie III*, one that has set records for both kinds of box office gross. What will your temptation be? Your temptation will be to think that however well-intentioned the folks running the school might be, the "tone" of the school is not nearly "high enough," and that all these families clearly have poor standards. You regret having to do this, but you are considering pulling your son, wrapping him up in cotton batting for two final semesters of Mom School.

You think the problem is low entertainment standards, when the actual problem is that no Christian parents—including you—are teaching their kids what moral leadership looks like. About a third of the kids who went to that movie didn't really want to, and wouldn't have gone if someone in the class—I am thinking of your son in particular—had done more than simply studied his shoelaces when the subject came up. You are tempted to think that the others have low entertainment standards, when the real lesson is that your son is not a moral leader. The response ought *not* to be to do something that will make him even less of one.

The Question of Craft Competence

Americans tend to be a pragmatic people, and if something doesn't work very well, it is tempting to point this out right at the start. And since government schooling in America is by and large an educational disaster area, it would have been easy to begin with this fact. The difficulty with applying this test to the secular government school system is that people can be persuaded to abandon those schools without truly understanding the foundational issues involved. And if we don't understand them, then we are simply reacting, not reforming. What we need is a *reformation* of education, built on biblical principles, and not a mere reaction from bad consequences.

Too many Christians have pulled their kids out of the government schools because there was one drug deal too many, or one condom in the classroom too many, or one academic scandal too many. This is fine if such episodes get parents to really think the issue through, but if it is just a superficial reaction, then the reformation we institute will be superficial as well. This is actually why too many Christian schools are just like the government schools of the 1950's—we got prayer and Bible reading back in, but everything else is largely unchanged. But this is like realizing that you are not enjoying a movie you rented, and so you skip back two scenes and try again. Or, to use a biblical metaphor, if we want different fruit, we need a different root.

At the same time, disobedience of God's ways does have negative consequences, and at some point we *should* notice them. If those hard consequences bring someone to his senses, that is all to the good. This is what happened in our Lord's story about the prodigal son—he was staring at the pig food, and the discrepancy between his condition and how the servants back home in his father's house were doing was borne in upon him. But we can easily imagine another story where someone simply pulled away from negative consequences temporarily—just in order to go back and try it again later. Maybe it will be different this time. But how many sins of compulsion have interludes of ineffective repentance?

Sin remains counterproductive. Jezebel led Israel into the worship of Baal, a Phoenician storm god. Among the Phoenicians, his consort was Astarte, a goddess of fertility and sexual love. As Israel began to worship "green," as it were, everything then turned mysteriously brown. YHWH was the true source of Israel's fertility and abundance—and it was not until *His* prophet Elijah gave the word that the rain came.

Whenever we place a created thing in the position that only God should have, it is not long before we have destroyed the blessing of that created thing. Men who pursue drunkenness soon lose their ability to enjoy wine. Men who chase after their sexual lusts are soon captive to them, and are then dragged down into sexual perversions. God has filled the world with good servants that make terrible masters. We have a similar situation with secular education. In the grip of rationalism, our schools have become havens of illiteracy and irrationalism. Secularists worship reason, and since this is one of the most unreasonable things a man can do, it is not surprising that we get abysmal results.

Now in one sense it is fully appropriate to take your kid out of a school when he is not learning how to read, in the same way that it would be reasonable to go get your car out of the shop if the gents there weren't fixing it. But so many children are being left uninstructed in schools that it is necessary to see that we would not do this with any other goods or services. Something *religious* is going on here. Eric Hoffer described the trajectory this way. First you have a movement, which turns into a business, which then is transformed into a racket. Government schools are now deeply in the racket phase. Because they are a racket, they are not performing their ostensible function—that of providing a rigorous education in the basics. In addition, they present a stumbling block for your child's soul. For these reasons, it is time to be done with them, but we must be done with them for the right reasons.

Every faithful Christian parent should want to know the *truth*, and not just the truth about ultimate things. A man can know the truth about Heaven and Hell, about the triune God, and about the vicarious death of Christ on the cross, and still not have the faintest idea about what he ought to be doing between now and next Thursday. A faithful Christian parent wants to know the truth about the task *he* has undertaken. Be diligent to know the state of your herds (Prov. 27:23). There is a very foolish school of thought when it comes to car maintenance and repair—"don't lift the hood if you don't want to know"—and this approach is *not* what we should be doing with regard to the education of the little ones in our charge. If your child is being mangled by the government school system, you should *want* to know this.

It is important to repeat again the principle that Paul sets out for us in the second letter to the Corinthians, which is that it is not enough to commend yourself, it is not enough to measure yourself by yourself, and it is not enough to compare yourself to those who are doing exactly the same thing you are doing. This is *not wise* (2 Cor. 10:12). The problem, the central problem, is *pedagogical ideology*, that which will brook no hard questions, and will tolerate no bringers of unpleasant truths. It is this attitude that is the enemy of small children, those who are not capable of resisting what is about to be done to them in the name of the latest thing.

So how then should we measure? When we are evaluating the pedagogical methods we are using, we have to be adults in our thinking. Remember the bell curve. The spread of innate educational ability will manifest itself over any population that is large enough—and private Christian schools, government schools, and the various forms of homeschooling (co-ops, on-line learning, and pure kitchen table homeschooling) are all large enough for us to start taking measurements—if we really want to.

No educational method should evaluated on the basis of the fact that there are kids bringing up the rear, and this includes the government schools. No educator can put in what God left out. But neither should we evaluate any method based simply on how the most gifted do. We all know the homeschoolers (I have met a number of them) who could get into Harvard three times before lunch. And at our local Christian School, Logos Academy, we have seen more than one class with academic abilities that I have described as "spooky." Also, taking the rough-cut numbers, about ten percent of the kids in the government schools are still competitive with anybody anywhere in the world. They can run with the big dogs—they have not been crippled (at least academically) by a failing school system.

The reason we should not evaluate the public schools by the performance of our best and brightest is that these are the kids who can teach themselves phonics by staring at milk cartons and cereal boxes. These are the kids with a robust immune system, which should never be taken as an argument for surrounding them with germs. There are a bunch of students bright enough to survive and excel despite the startling incompetence of everyone around them. This is no reason for the team of incompetents around them to start giving one another teaching awards.

Taking the long view, an educational system or method should be evaluated on the basis of two basic goals—its ability to thoroughly educate the large majority of students in the fat part of the bell curve, and to do so in a way that simultaneously teaches and enables the best and brightest without exasperating them. I am not just speaking of academics; *children have souls*. It is here that the government school system is entirely failing.

One more point should be made. The desire to evade accountability and unpleasant job reviews is a fallen *human* desire. We are all of us sons of Adam, and we all need the truth. Paul tells the Romans that they should not be conformed to the world, but rather to to be transformed by the renewal of their minds (Rom. 12:1–2). What is the immediate result of such a transformation? "For by the grace given to me I say to everyone among you not to think of himself more highly than he ought to think, but to think with sober judgment, each according to the measure of faith that God has assigned" (Rom. 12:3). Self-flattery is a temptation that comes to all those who live in this world. Seeing yourself and your activities accurately is one of the greatest gifts of God's grace that He can bestow, and He wants to bestow it on all of us—and all of us need it. I have been on educational boards of various descriptions for over thirty years, and have visited more schools around the country than I could possibly remember. Also, I have been a pastor of hundreds of homeschooled and privately-schooled kids over the course of decades. I have seen the disastrous results of government education. I am been a close observer of all these things. If your children are in the government school system, and if you are in a position to do something about it, *I would plead with you to do so.*

Get To and Got To

Having made this plea, there is one more thing. Conservative Christians have standards, and we are going to stick to them, by golly. And that is actually a good thing, so long as we are sticking to them. The problem arises when they start sticking to us, as when cheat grass gets in your socks.

The principle I have in mind affects all sorts of issues—attendance at worship, sabbath keeping, entertainment standards, biblical courtship, and so on, down the block and around the corner. Our subject here is Christian education. I am not talking about bogus legalisms, like prohibitions of processed foods in the name of Jesus, but rather issues for which an actual biblical case could be made, as I believe has been made with regard to Christian education. But the fact that the standard is stoutly biblical doesn't keep us from picking it up by the wrong end. God's standards—all His true standards—are all a *get to*, not a *got to*. Though surely, someone will say, there is an obligatory *got to* element in there? Sure, but we can only see it that way when we are holding it upside down.

Christian kids should receive a Christian education. The letter kills, and *true* letters, being as sharp as they are, kill the very best. The letter stirs up a disinclination to do whatever it is, even if that thing is the coolest thing in the world (Rom. 3:20; 5:20). The law, understood this way, chases us away from the good. But the law, understood as the grace of God, blesses us beyond all measure.

Now, all of this is the prelude to my invitation to a thoroughly Christian education. Thoroughly Christian education is entirely a good thing, and it is something required (got to!) by the terms of a genuine Christian worldview. If some do not see the blessing that it represents (as some do not), there is a pressing temptation on the part of those who do see it to try to motivate the others by an appeal to raw obligation at the individual level. That doesn't work. It is counterproductive. It stirs up unnecessary resistance. People can't be chased into a sense of *get to* by constantly reminding them how much they have *got to*. Christian education is grace, not law. It is grace for your children, not law for your children. It is grace for you, not law for you.

The Lord of Tomorrow Morning

Fleetwood Mac exhorted us all plainly, "Don't stop thinking about tomorrow." Well, okay. And politicians consistently tell us that they want to be elected so that they can build a bridge to the future—as though we could go anywhere else, whether we build that bridge or not. But behind these bromides is a serious point that men have to *try* to address. As God's creatures, we occupy space and we live in time. As those who live in time, we need to develop a solid and biblical theology of the future.

We need a theology of time (which includes a theology of the future) because we are not here simply to mark time. If God has given us resources and opportunities, as He most certainly has, it is not safe or right to bury them in the ground, hoping to give them back to God interest-free. People who do that think that God is a hard master. By a theology of time and history, I mean more than an optimistic eschatology, although that is an important component of what I mean.

What happens in time? Among other things crops grow to the harvest. Money matures with interest. *Children grow to adulthood*. Institutions grow and mature. But it is also true that crops fail and wither. Money disappears in stock collapses. Children can get stuck in perpetual adolescence. So in all true growth, it is necessary to cross new thresholds periodically. To stop growing is to die, whether the death happens that very instant or not.

So you have decided to embark on the arduous task of providing a true Christian education for your children. Are you doing what *cannot* succeed unless God blesses it in His grace? We should acknowledge that up front. What else is new? There is no appreciable difference between ceasing to swim up the river, and floating down the river. Faithfulness is always to be found *in the next thing*. Put another way, faithfulness is in the future.

> Shasta's heart fainted at these words for he felt he had no strength left. And he writhed inside at what seemed the cruelty and unfairness of the demand. He had not yet learned that if you do one good deed your reward usually is to be set to do another and harder and better one. But all he said out loud was: "Where is the King?" (C. S. Lewis, *The Horse and His Boy*)

This should not be taken as the cynic would take it—in the sense that no good deed goes unpunished—but it does help to explain where we are. The carnal heart wants to do a certain number of good deeds, get them safely in the bank, and then trust in that bank. But the just will live by faith, and hope that is seen is no hope at all, as the apostle teaches in Romans 8. Hope that is well in hand is not hope.

In the task of bringing the entire world to submit to the kindness of Christ's authority, His easy and light yoke, there is much work to be done—is there not? And in order to accomplish that work, we must be oriented to the future, set on the next thing. Our desire this moment is to be faithful today and tomorrow, not yesterday and today.

This means your children. That is what it means in today's tomorrow. Not next year's tomorrow, or the next generation's. We are here today, on the threshold of a new generation of Christian students. We are here because we want to be faithful to the Lord Jesus, and because Jesus is the Lord of all things. And if He is the Lord of all things, then He is the Lord of tomorrow morning.